Shake it Up Every Day
40-6185

Designs by Jean Kievlan

Published by Provo Craft
285 E. 900 South, Provo, Utah 84606

Managing Editor - Clella Gustin
Design and Book Coordinator - Barbara Sanderson
Graphic Art - Pam Gregg   Photography - Craig Young

Also in this series
"Shake it up for the Holidays"
#40-6186

The projects in this book are designed to provide ideas. In most cases, other brands of acrylic paint, glass paint, glass etching products, felt, doll hair and trims will work equally as well as the products used. Mix, match and use whatever you have at hand or is readily available.

Provo Craft stock numbers are listed for the glass shakers. The other products used in this book are available at your local craft or variety store from these companies:

Americana Acrylic Paint and Ultra Gloss Enamels:
DECOART
Hwy Jct 150 & 27, Stanford, KY 40484

Small Wood Parts:
LARA'S CRAFTS
590 N. Beach Street, Fort Worth, TX 76111

ZIG® Fine Tip Millennium and Opaque Markers:
EK SUCCESS
611 Industrial Road, Carlstadt, NJ 07072

Felt:
CPE, 541 W Springs Hwy, Union, SC 29379

Etchall® Dip'n Etch and Etching Creme:
B & B PRODUCTS, INC.
18700 N. 107th Ave. #13, Sun City, AZ 85373

Doll Hair:
ONE AND ONLY CREATIONS
P. O. Box 2370, Napa, CA 94558

Paint Brushes
ROYAL BRUSH MFG., INC.
6949 Kennedy Ave., Hammond, IN 46323

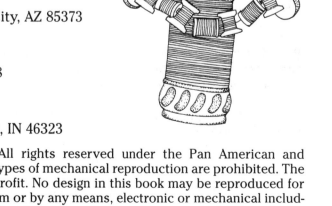

ISBN 1-58050-054-4

3

Basic Tips and Instructions For Shaker Pals

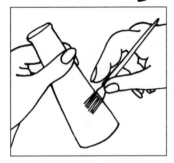

1. Paint glass with DecoArt Ultra Gloss Enamels if desired, following manufacturer's instructions. Or, glass may be etched, then painted with regular acrylics. I prefer this method since the etched surface is easy to paint and the patterns may be traced right onto etched glass using graphite paper if needed. Two coats of most colors of acrylic paint cover quite nicely. Let each coat of paint dry thoroughly before applying the next. Seal areas painted with acrylic paints with a light spray of Krylon Matte Finish, or a coat of water based sealer. Note: Do not seal etched (frosted) areas with sealer or Matte Finish or they will disappear! For special tips on etching or painting on glass, see page 5.

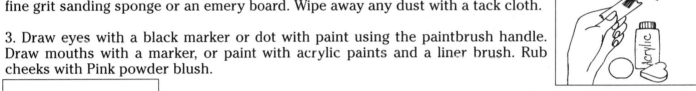

2. Paint wood pieces with Decoart Americana Acrylics. Most small wood parts require little or no sanding. If necessary, any rough edges can be smoothed with a fine grit sanding sponge or an emery board. Wipe away any dust with a tack cloth.

3. Draw eyes with a black marker or dot with paint using the paintbrush handle. Draw mouths with a marker, or paint with acrylic paints and a liner brush. Rub cheeks with Pink powder blush.

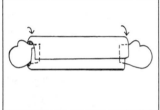

4. Create tube arms using a mini mitten or split egg and a piece of felt. To create a tube arm, apply lo-temp glue around wrist, then position hand on felt as shown in illustration. Bring felt up over wrist then press into glue. Apply glue to opposite end of felt, then bring felt down over wrist and press in place. Repeat for other hand. Glue remainder of felt tube shut. Hint: You may glue a chenille stem or piece of wire inside the sleeve for added support if you wish to position the arms.

5. Create single arms in the same manner as the tube arms. Trim the top edge of the felt to round it, then apply a drop of glue inside the top of the sleeve to close it.

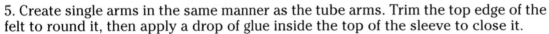
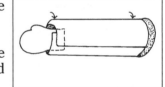

6. Glue tube arms at the back of the metal shaker top with lo-temp glue. Glue single arms at the sides of the shaker top, or to the shaker top which has been covered with a strip of felt.

7. Create capes, jackets and gathered aprons using patterns provided. Gather top edge with short running stitches using a needle and thread. Bring tube arms through armhole slits. Single arms are glued directly into the armhole slits, or in some cases directly to the outside of the cape or jacket.

8. Glue round and square collars directly onto the metal cap, making sure that the lo-temp glue does not drip onto glass. Glue felt collar or body strips around the metal cap. Glue top edge of felt to top of cap, easing fullness around cap as shown in the illustration.

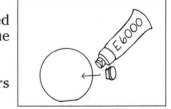

9. Attach the head to the metal cap or felt collar with lo-temp glue. It is suggested that ears, noses and other wood parts attached be glued to the head with Goop glue or E-6000 glue for maximum hold.

10. Attach embellishments such as felt, doll hair, ribbons, buttons and silk flowers with lo-temp glue.

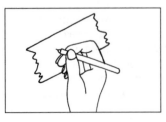

11. Write sayings on wood signs with ZIG .03 Black Millennium marker.

12. Write sayings on glass using ZIG Fine Tip Opaque Markers.

13. Special Tip: Use a pair of heavy duty scissors to cut ½" hearts in half for ears. When you cut the heart in half, one side will usually split so it's best to have one heart to cut for each ear.

Instructions For Etching Glass

MATERIALS NEEDED:

Glass Shaker

Plastic Container as Tall and Wide as the Shaker

Etchall Dip'n Etch or Etching Cream

Black Marker

1. Remove cap from shaker. Fill shaker with water then place in plastic container. Fill plastic container with water until desired level is reached for etching. Remove shaker from water. Mark water level on outside of plastic container with a Black marker then pour water from plastic container. Dry outside of shaker and inside of container with a paper towel.

2. Refill plastic container with Dip'n Etch. Carefully place water filled shaker back into the plastic container with the etching solution. Let shaker sit in solution for 15 minutes. Remove shaker then wash thoroughly under running water. Dry shaker to see the wonderful etched surface! You can leave the shaker just as it is, or paint it with acrylic paints. Don't forget to pour the Dip'n Etch back into the jar to be used again and again!

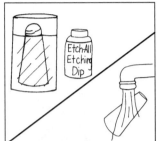

3. You can also etch glass with Etching Creme. This technique works best on square containers, but you can also etch round containers. Work on a protected surface or a plastic plate. Apply the Etching Creme to the glass thickly with a squeegee making sure to cover all of the surface to be etched. Let creme sit 15 minutes then use the squeegee to scrape the creme back into the jar (it can be used again and again). Rinse off shaker thoroughly under running water. Note: Special effects can be created with etching creme using sponges or using a fine tip applicator to apply the etching creme.

Special Tips for Painting on Glass

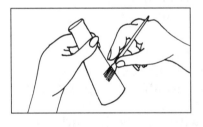

1. Glass to be painted should be clean and free of oil and dirt. Follow the instructions for etching glass if painting with acrylic paints. Whether painting with acrylic paints or Ultra Gloss Enamels, use a wide, flat brush to basecoat surfaces. If you want an opaque look, several coats of paint may be required with some colors. Apply one even coat then let dry thoroughly. Apply a second coat or third coat as necessary. Let paint dry thoroughly before painting additional designs.

2. Use round brushes to fill in smaller areas or to make leaves or flowers. Use a liner brush to paint lines and details. If using Ultra Gloss Enamels, allow paint to cure for 24 hours before adding further embellishments.

**Provo Craft offers a wide variety of glass shakers
and glass containers including ornaments, cookie jars, boutique jars & more!
Just think of all the fun things you can make with a little paint and some imagination!**

Cheerleader

DECOART AMERICANA PAINTS:
Fleshtone

GLASS SHAKER:
Provo Craft #20-4212

WOOD SHAPES:
One 1¼" Doll Head
Two 1⅜" x ¾" Mini Mittens

OTHER SUPPLIES:
Felt (White, Cardinal and Gold)
  or colors of your choice
Lil'Loopies Doll Hair - Rust
ZIG .03 Black Millennium Marker
Lo Temp Glue
Pink Powder Blush
Thread
Optional: Pink Jelly Beans

INSTRUCTIONS:
1. Paint head and hands Fleshtone. Dot eyes with Black marker then rub cheeks with powder blush.
2. Glue a 1½" x 5" strip of White felt around the metal top, easing fullness of felt around lid top. Glue head in place. Glue a ¼" strip of Cardinal felt around the bottom of the doll head as a collar.

3. Create sleeves as shown in illustration using a 2½" x 2" long piece of White felt for each arm. Glue an arm at each side of the doll.
4. Using patterns provided, cut the megaphone of Cardinal and Gold felt. Glue it to the front of the doll. Cut eight strips of Gold and of Cardinal felt measuring ¾" x 1¾". Glue the short ends of the Gold strips around the glass shaker right under bottom edge of the felt covered shaker top. Overlap, then glue the Cardinal strips over the Gold strips.
5. Cut pieces of Gold and Cardinal felt 1½" square. Cut fringe ⅛" apart to within ¼" of the end. Pinch the top edges together then tie with thread. Glue the pom-pom shaker in the doll's hand.
6. Wrap doll hair around a 2¾" piece of cardboard until center is about ¾" wide. Cut one end of hair to remove from cardboard. Tie a piece of hair around the center of the bundle. Glue hair on head. Arrange in pigtails using another strand of hair to tie each pigtail. Cut a few bangs in front if desired.
7. Optional: Fill container with Pink jelly beans.

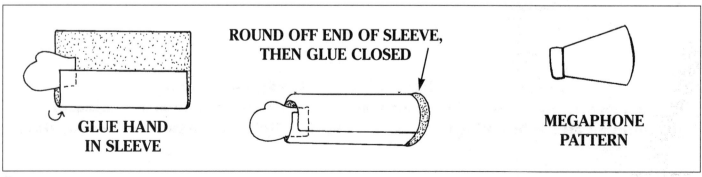

**GLUE HAND
IN SLEEVE**

**ROUND OFF END OF SLEEVE,
THEN GLUE CLOSED**

**MEGAPHONE
PATTERN**

Football Player

DECOART AMERICANA PAINTS:
Burnt Umber
Cranberry Wine
Fleshtone
Lamp Black
Raw Sienna
True Ochre

GLASS SHAKER:
Provo Craft #20-4210

WOOD SHAPES:
One 1¼" Ball Head
Two 1⅜" x ¾" Mittens
Football

OTHER SUPPLIES:
Etchall Dip'n Etch or Etching Creme
Felt (Champagne, Cardinal and Gold)
Dark Brown Wavy Wool Hair
2" Gold Plastic Football Helmet
Pink Powder Blush
ZIG .03 Black Millennium Marker
Lo-Temp Glue

INSTRUCTIONS:
1. Etch shaker following basic instructions for etching glass. Paint etched glass Cranberry Wine. Paint ⅜" wide True Ochre stripes down each side of the body. Shade the leg area and paint the shoes with Lamp Black.
2. Paint the football Raw Sienna. Shade details on the ball with Burnt Umber. Draw lacing lines with the Black marker.
3. Paint head and hands Fleshtone. Dot eyes with Black marker then rub cheeks with blush.
4. Cut a 2¼" x 5" piece of felt. Position the felt so that ¼" extends above the metal top and the 2" covers the sides of the top and extends down past the metal top. Glue the strip around the metal top. Ease the fullness of felt around the metal top then glue in place. Glue the head on the metal top.
5. Create two arms using a 2½" x 2" piece of Champagne felt for each. Cut a sleeve of Gold felt for each arm that measures 1" x 2½". Glue the sleeve over the top part of the Champagne felt arm. Round off the top part of the sleeve, then glue closed. Glue a sleeve at each side of the felt covered metal top.
6 Cut a Cardinal 'T' then glue it at the front of the shirt. Glue a thin strip of Cardinal felt around the neck as a collar. Glue the football in the hands.
7. Glue the hair then the helmet on the head.

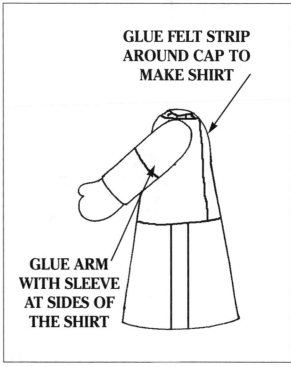

GLUE FELT STRIP AROUND CAP TO MAKE SHIRT

GLUE ARM WITH SLEEVE AT SIDES OF THE SHIRT

Potpourri Angel

DECOART AMERICANA PAINTS:
Fleshtone
Titanium White

GLASS SHAKER:
Provo Craft #20-4206

WOOD SHAPES:
One 1¼" Doll Head
Two 1½" x ⅛" Hearts (Wings)

OTHER SUPPLIES:
4" White Crocheted Doily
¼" Blue Button
8" of ¹⁄₁₆" Metallic Gold Ribbon
Lil'Loopies Doll Hair - Blonde
Lo-Temp Glue
Pink Powder Blush
ZIG .03 Black Millennium Marker
Optional: Potpourri

INSTRUCTIONS:
1. Paint head Fleshtone. Dot eyes with Black marker. Rub cheeks with blush.
2. Paint hearts Titanium White.
3. Remove the metal top then fill shaker with potpourri. Hand feed larger pieces of potpourri through the opening.
4. Glue the doily over the top of the shaker. Glue the head on the doily.
5. Glue the doll hair on the head, then the heart wings at the back of the head and the shaker.
6. Glue a Gold bow then a button at the front of the collar. Glue the shaker top on the head.

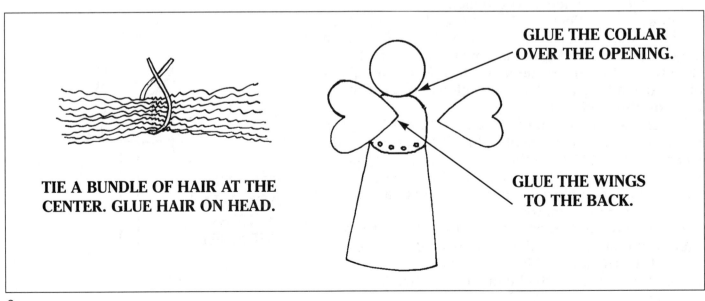

TIE A BUNDLE OF HAIR AT THE CENTER. GLUE HAIR ON HEAD.

GLUE THE COLLAR OVER THE OPENING.

GLUE THE WINGS TO THE BACK.

Baby Girl

DECOART AMERICANA PAINTS:
Fleshtone
Napa Red
Titanium White

GLASS SHAKER:
Provo Craft #20-4212

WOOD SHAPES:
One 1¼" Doll Head
Two 1⅜" x ¾" Mini Mittens
One 1¾" x 1¼" Gingerbread Boy

OTHER SUPPLIES:
Felt (Champagne and Pink)
5" of 2" Wide Flat White Lace
Blonde Mini Curl Doll Hair
Plastic Earring Back (Pacifier)
2" x 2½" Piece of Quilt or Patchwork Fabric
ZIG .03 Black Millennium Marker
6" of Pink Embroidery Floss
Needle and White Thread
Lo-Temp Glue
Pink Powder Blush
Optional: Cotton Swabs

INSTRUCTIONS:
1. Paint head and hands Fleshtone. Paint head, hands and feet of baby doll Fleshtone. Paint the sleeper with Napa Red lightened with Titanium White. Shade sleeper with Napa Red. Dot and draw eyes on the faces with Black marker. Rub cheeks with blush. Dot baby doll's mouth with Napa Red.
2. Create tube sleeves using a 2½" x 5½" piece of Champagne felt. Glue head on shaker top. Glue center of arms at back of shaker top.
3. Using pattern provided, cut a bib of Pink Felt. Glue bib at neck. Glue hair on head and pacifier at mouth. Glue quilt in hand then doll to other hand and quilt. Glue a Pink embroidery floss bow at side of neck.
4. Gather one long edge of the flat lace. Pull up thread tightly then tie off. Gather bonnet again, more loosely this time, ¾" from scalloped edge. Tie off threads then glue bonnet on head.
Optional: Fill jar with cotton swabs.

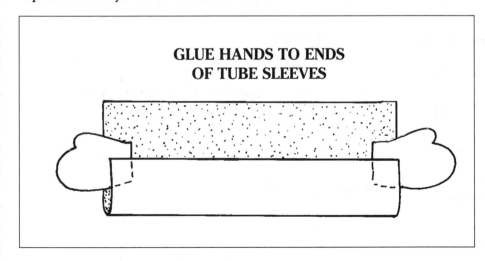

**GLUE HANDS TO ENDS
OF TUBE SLEEVES**

BIB PATTERN

Sweet Ballerina

DECOART AMERICANA PAINTS:
Fleshtone
Mauve
Dazzling Metallics Champagne Gold

GLASS SHAKER:
Provo Craft #20-4210

WOOD SHAPES:
One 1¼" Doll Head
One ¾" x ¾" Primitive Star

OTHER SUPPLIES:
Pink Felt
Lil'Loopies Doll Hair - Blonde
4" Piece of 1" Wide Mauve Satin Ribbon
6" Piece of ⅛" Rose Satin Ribbon
Two 3" x 18" Pieces of Fine Pink Tulle
6" Piece of ¹⁄₁₆" Metallic Gold Ribbon or Floss
ZIG .03 Black Millennium Marker
Lo-Temp Glue
Pink Powder Blush
Needle and Pink Thread
Optional: Pink Jelly Beans

INSTRUCTIONS:
1. Etch shaker following basic instructions for etching glass. After etching, paint the bottom ⅔ of the shaker Fleshtone and the top ⅓ Mauve.
2. Paint the head Fleshtone and the star Champagne Gold. Dot the eyes with Black marker then rub cheeks with blush.
3. Glue the Mauve ribbon around the metal cap, easing fullness at the top. Glue head on metal top.
4. Fold a ¾" x 5" piece of Pink felt in half widthwise to create the arms. Glue raw edges together. Glue edges of arms at back of ribbon covered top. Glue the star in the hands.
5. Fold a piece of 3" X 18" tulle in half widthwise. Gather along fold with short running stitches. Glue one layer of gathered tulle on glass shaker. Repeat procedure with remaining strip of tulle.
6. Tie the Gold ribbon around the doll's neck. Glue the button below the ribbon. Glue a bundle of doll hair on the head. Bring ends to top of head, then tie ribbon around hair to create a topknot.

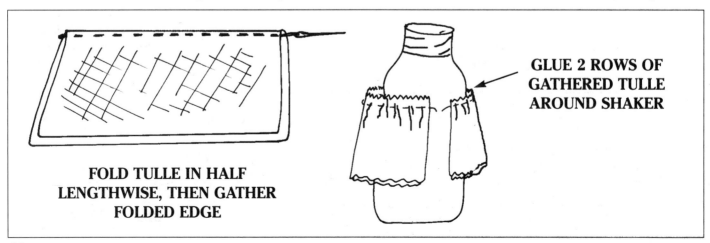

FOLD TULLE IN HALF LENGTHWISE, THEN GATHER FOLDED EDGE

GLUE 2 ROWS OF GATHERED TULLE AROUND SHAKER

Cookie Gourmet

DECOART AMERICANA PAINTS:
Antique White
Burnt Umber
Dove Grey
Fleshtone
Primary Red
Raw Sienna
Titanium White

GLASS SHAKER:
Provo Craft #20-4207

WOOD SHAPES:
One 1¼" Doll Head
Two 1⅜" x ¾" Mini Mittens
One 1¼" x 1¼" Wing (Mustache)
One 1½" x ⅛" Circle
Five Axle Caps (Cookies)
One Mini Rolling Pin
One 1⁹⁄₁₆" x 1⅜" Candle Cup (Hat)

OTHER SUPPLIES:
Etchall Dip'n Etch or Etching Creme
Felt (Champagne, Red and White)
White Mini Curl Doll Hair
ZIG .03 Black Millennium Marker
Lo-Temp and Goop Glue
Pink Powder Blush

INSTRUCTIONS:
1. Etch shaker following basic instructions for etching glass. Paint the etched shaker, candle cup and mustache Titanium White. Shade leg line, mustache, hat brim and gathers with Dove Grey.
2. Paint head and hands Fleshtone. Dot eyes with Black marker. Rub cheeks with blush.
3. Wash circle with water thinned Raw Sienna. Paint axle caps Antique White. Dry brush the tops with Raw Sienna then dot with Burnt Umber. Paint handles of rolling pin with Primary Red.
4. Glue a 1¼" x 5" piece of Champagne felt around the metal cap easing fullness at top of cap. Glue head on cap.
5. Create tube sleeves with a 2½" wide x 6" long piece of White felt. Glue center of tube at back of neck. Glue a 4" x 4" x 5" Red felt triangle around the neck as a scarf.
6. Glue hair, mustache and hat on head. Glue cookies and rolling pin on tray, then the tray in the hands.

**GLUE HANDS
TO ENDS OF SLEEVES**

12

Button Seamstress

DECOART AMERICANA PAINTS:
Fleshtone

GLASS SHAKER:
Provo Craft #20-4212

WOOD SHAPES:
One 1¼" Doll Head
Two 1⅜" x ¾" Mini Mittens
Three ½" x ½" Spools

OTHER SUPPLIES:
Pink Felt
Lil'Loopies Doll Hair - Blonde
4" White Crocheted Doily
Three ¼" Blue Buttons
Pink, Blue and Green Embroidery Floss
Gold Metallic Thread
Four ⅝" x ¾" Pieces of White Cardstock
ZIG .03 Black Millennium Marker
Lo-Temp Glue
Pink Powder Blush
Optional: Buttons to Fill Shaker

FLOSS HOLDER PATTERN

INSTRUCTIONS:

1. Paint head and hands Fleshtone. Dot eyes with Black marker then rub cheeks with blush. Cut a triangular shaped wedge from the doily which includes two scallops. Glue the remainder of the doily to the metal cap as a collar then glue the head on top. Glue a Pink floss bow and a Blue button on the collar.
2. Wrap the center area of the shaker with Pink embroidery floss. Wrap spools with Pink, Blue and Green floss or thread. Cut four floss holders from cardstock using the pattern provided then wrap each one with Gold thread.
3. Create tube arms using a 2½" x 5" Piece of felt. Glue arms at back of cap.
4. Wrap doll hair around a 2¾" piece of cardboard until center is about ¾" wide. Cut one end of hair to remove from cardboard. Tie a piece of hair around the center of the bundle. Glue hair on head. Arrange in pigtails using another strand of hair to tie each pigtail. Cut a few bangs in front if desired. Glue a Blue button at each pigtail.
5. String spools on a piece of Pink floss. Tie ends of floss to each arm. Glue Gold floss cards onto the garland.
Optional: Fill shaker with buttons.

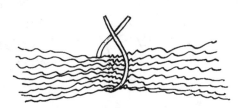

TIE A BUNDLE OF HAIR AT THE CENTER. GLUE HAIR ON HEAD, THEN TIE INTO PIGTAILS

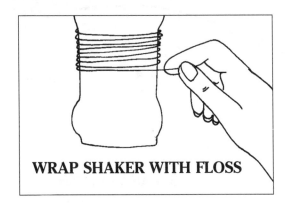

WRAP SHAKER WITH FLOSS

'Clowning Around'

DECOART AMERICANA PAINTS:
Cadmium Yellow
Lamp Black
Primary Red
Sapphire
Titanium White

GLASS SHAKER:
Provo Craft #20-4208

WOOD SHAPES:
One 1¼" Doll Head
Two 1⅜" x ¾" Mini Mittens
Three ¾" Beads (Balloons)
One ¼" Birch Roundhead Plug (Nose)
Two ⅞" Split Wren Eggs (Feet)

OTHER SUPPLIES:
Felt (Yellow and Royal Blue)
Auburn Wavy Wool Hair
Three Pieces of Tan Chenille Stem (2¾", 3" and 3½")
Two ⅜" Gold Jingle Bells
6" of ⅛" Red Ribbon
Lo-Temp and Goop Glue
Pink Powder Blush
Optional: Candy Coated Chocolates

INSTRUCTIONS:
1. Paint head and hands Titanium White. Paint 'star' pattern on eye Sapphire and mouth Primary Red. Dot eye with Titanium White. Let paint dry, then dot pupil with Lamp Black. Paint eyebrows Black. Line a leg line in the center just above where the feet will be attached.
2. Paint split eggs, one bead and nose Primary Red. Paint one of the remaining beads Sapphire and one Cadmium Yellow.
3. Cut collar of Yellow felt. Glue collar on metal cap. Create arms using a 2½" x 2" piece of Royal Blue felt for each arm. Glue arms at sides of metal cap.
4. Glue chenille stems into bead holes. Tie the Red ribbon around the stems, then glue the balloon bundle in clown's hands. Glue jingle bells on collar and wavy wool hair on head.
5. Use Goop glue to attach nose to face.

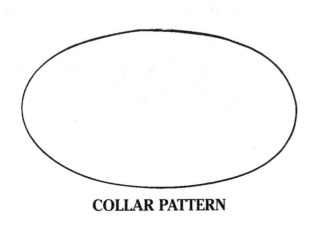

COLLAR PATTERN

GLUE SHOES TO THE FRONT OF THE SHAKER WITH GOOP GLUE.

14

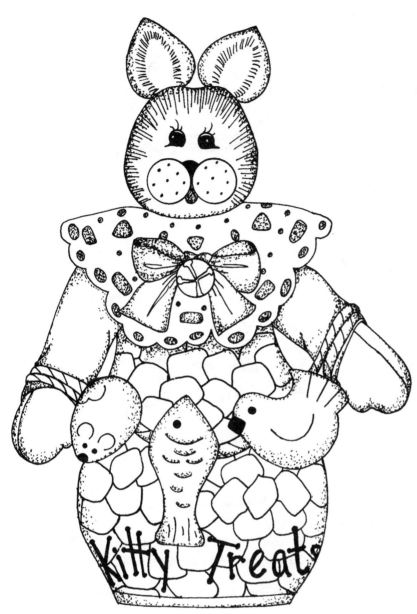

Kitty Treats

DECOART AMERICANA PAINTS:

Antique White	Burnt Umber
Blue Grey Mist	Lamp Black
Primary Red	Raw Sienna
Viridian Green	Raspberry
Sapphire	Titanium White
Cadmium Yellow	

GLASS SHAKER:
Provo Craft #20-4209

WOOD SHAPES:
One 1¼" x 1⅜" Crab Apple
Two 1⅜" x ¾" Mini Mittens
Two ¾" x 1" Hearts (Ears)
Two Axle Caps (Cheeks)
One ⅞" Split Wren Egg (Mouse)
One 1" x 1⅛" Dove
One 1" x 2½" Fish

OTHER SUPPLIES:
2½" x 6" Piece of Grey Felt
4" White Crocheted Doily
⅜" Gold Jingle Bell
10" Piece of Jute
⅝" x 8" Piece of Green Fabric
ZIG .03 Black Millennium Marker
ZIG White Opaque Marker
1" Piece of Heavy Duty Grey Thread
   (Mouse's Tail)
Lo-Temp and Goop Glue
Pink Powder Blush
Optional: Kitty Treats

INSTRUCTIONS:
1. Paint paws, head and ears Antique White. Dry brush with Blue Grey Mist, then Raw Sienna and finally Burnt Umber on all Antique White pieces to create fur effect.
2. Wash inner ear with water-thinned Raspberry. Shade inner ear edge with Raspberry.
3. Paint nose Raspberry and mouth Primary Red. Dot eyes Black then highlight with White. Use Black marker to draw eyelashes.
4. Paint cheeks (axle caps) Titanium White. Dot with Black marker.
6. Paint mouse Blue Grey Mist. Dot nose Raspberry. Draw details with Black marker.
7. Paint fish White. Shade lower edge with Raspberry and upper edge with Viridian Green. Draw details with Black marker.
8. Paint bird Sapphire. Shade chest with Primary Red. Highlight wing and tail feathers with Titanium White. Paint beak Cadmium Yellow. Dot eye Lamp Black.
9. Create tube arms using the Grey felt. Dry brush the felt with Raw Sienna and Burnt Umber.
10. Glue the tube arms at the back of the shaker lid then glue the collar over the lid. Glue a Green fabric bow and the jingle bell on the collar.
11. Glue the cheeks and ears to the head with Goop glue. Glue the head on the collar. Glue mouse, fish and bird to the jute garland then glue the garland around the wrists. Glue a Grey thread tail on the mouse.

Going Fishin'

DECOART AMERICANA PAINTS:

Fleshtone   Blue Grey Mist   Khaki Tan
Plantation Pine   Raw Sienna   Raspberry
Forest Green   Titanium White
Hauser Medium Green

GLASS SHAKER:
Provo Craft #20-4208

WOOD SHAPES:
One 1¼" Doll Head   Two 1⅜" x ¾" Mini Mittens
One 1" x 2½" Fish   1" x ¹³⁄₁₆" Candle Cup (Pail)
¼" Birch Roundhead Plug (Nose)

OTHER SUPPLIES:
Etchall Dip'n Etch
Felt (Sage Green and Wheat)
Mini Curls Doll Hair - Brown
4" Piece of ¼" Dowel
10" of Jute (fish line and pail handle)
ZIG .03 Black Millennium Marker
Lo-Temp Glue
Pink Powder Blush
Needle and Green Thread

**HAT BRIM
PATTERN**

INSTRUCTIONS:
1. Etch shaker following basic instructions for etching glass.
After etching, paint the bottom ½ of the shaker Hauser Medium Green and the top ½ Khaki Tan. Shade the Khaki Tan areas with Raw Sienna. Shade along the glass impressions on the bottom of the shaker with Plantation Pine.
2. Paint the head and hands Fleshtone. Paint the nose Raspberry. Dot the eyes with Black marker then rub the cheeks with blush.
3. Paint the pail Blue Grey Mist. Paint the fish Titanium White. Shade bottom of fish with Raspberry and top of fish with Forest Green. Draw details on fish with Black marker.
4. Glue a 1" x 4" piece of Wheat felt around the metal top easing fullness over the top as you glue. Create two arms using a 2½" x 2" piece of Wheat felt for each.
5. Glue nose on head then head on metal top. Glue arms at sides. Glue hair on head.
6. Cut ¼" wide strips of sage felt then glue strips separately onto body and top as shown in the illustration. Glue jute on pole and bucket.
7. Create hat using a 1¼ x 4½" piece of Sage Green felt. Gather felt on one long edge, pull up gathers tightly then tie off. Glue edges shut at back. Turn hat inside out. Cut a double brim of Sage Green felt using the pattern provided. Glue the brim on hat then glue the hat on the head.
8. Glue the fish to the end of the jute, glue the pole into his left arm and glue the bucket to his right arm.

**GLUE FELT
STRIPS
SEPARATELY
ON TOP AND
ON BODY.**

Hogs and Kisses

DECOART AMERICANA PAINTS:
Buttermilk
Fleshtone
French Mocha
Lamp Black
Titanium White
Milk Chocolate

GLASS SHAKER:
Provo Craft #20-4209

WOOD SHAPES:
One 1½" Doll Head
Two ⅞" Split Wren Eggs (Hands)
Two ¾" x 1" Hearts (Ears)
One ¾" x 3½" Ribbon Banner
One Axle Cap (Nose)

OTHER SUPPLIES:
Camel Colored Felt
¾" x 8" Piece of Red/Ecru Check Fabric
ZIG .03 Black Millennium Marker
Lo -Temp Glue
Pink Powder Blush
Optional: Foil Wrapped Chocolate Kisses

INSTRUCTIONS:
1. Paint head, ears, and hands Fleshtone. Paint hooves with Milk Chocolate. Paint nose and shade ears with French Mocha.
2. Dot eyes with White. Dot pupils and nostrils with Lamp Black. Rub cheeks with blush. Draw a mouth with Black marker.
3. Paint banner Buttermilk. Shade with Milk Chocolate. Write 'Hogs & Kisses' with Black marker.
4. Create tube arms using a 2½" x 6" Piece of Camel felt. Glue arms at back of metal top. Glue the banner to the hands.
5. Glue nose and ears on head, then head on metal top. Glue a fabric bow at the front of the chin.
Optional: Fill container with chocolate candies.

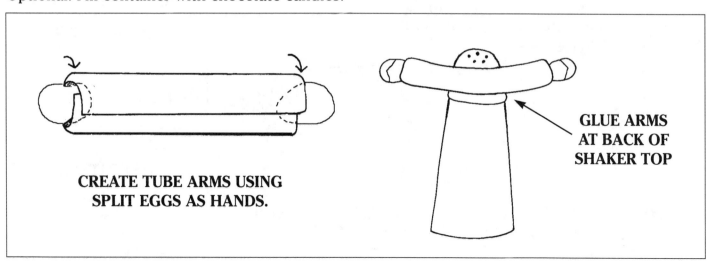

CREATE TUBE ARMS USING SPLIT EGGS AS HANDS.

GLUE ARMS AT BACK OF SHAKER TOP

Nurses Have Heart

DECOART AMERICANA PAINTS:
Fleshtone
Titanium White

GLASS SHAKER:
Provo Craft #20-4210

WOOD SHAPES:
One 1¼" Doll Head
Two 1⅜" x ¾" Mini Mittens
One ½" x ⅛" Heart
One 1" Square (³⁄₁₆" Thick)

OTHER SUPPLIES:
Felt (White and Red)
Brown Mini Curls Doll Hair
ZIG .03 Black Millennium Marker
Lo-Temp Glue
Pink Powder Blush
Optional: White Breath Mints

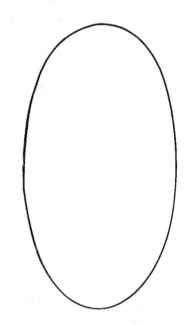

COLLAR PATTERN

INSTRUCTIONS:
1. Paint head and hands Fleshtone. Dot eyes with Black marker. Rub cheeks with blush.
2. Paint the square Titanium White. Write the saying on the square with the Black marker.
3. Paint the heart Red. Glue the heart on the square.
4. Cut a collar of White felt. Glue collar over metal top. Glue head on collar.
5. Create two arms using a 2½" x 2" piece of White felt for each. Glue the arms at the sides of the metal top. Glue the square with the heart in one hand.
6. Cut a 1½" x 2" piece of White felt for the hat. Fold felt in half, then glue sides together as shown in the illustration. Cut a white felt brim for the hat then glue it across the front. Glue a ⅛" strip of Red felt across the brim.
7. Glue the hair, then the hat on the head.
8. Cut a cross of Red felt then glue it to the collar.
Optional: Fill the container with White breath mints

BRIM PATTERN

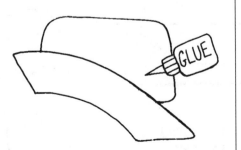

FOLD HAT IN HALF THEN GLUE SIDES TOGETHER.

GLUE BRIM ACROSS FRONT OF HAT.

HAT PATTERN

Puppy Treats

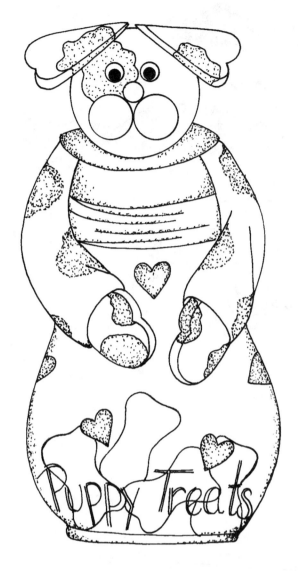

DECOART AMERICANA PAINTS:
Antique White
Honey Brown
Lamp Black
Milk Chocolate
Titanium White

GLASS SHAKER:
Provo Craft #20-4209

WOOD SHAPES:
One 1½" Doll Head
Two 1⅜" x ¾" Mini Mittens (Paws)
Two Axle Caps (Muzzle)
Two ½" x 1" Primitive Hearts (Ears)
One ¼" Birch Roundhead Plug (Nose)

OTHER SUPPLIES:
Felt (Wheat and Red)
ZIG Red and White Opaque Markers
Lo-Temp and Goop Glue
Pink Powder Blush
Optional: Small Dog Biscuits

INSTRUCTIONS:
1. Paint paws, head and ears Honey Brown. Shade edges and paint spots with Milk Chocolate. Paint nose Milk Chocolate and muzzle pieces Antique White.
2. Dot eyes White. When dry, dot pupils with Lamp Black. Rub cheeks with blush. Glue ears, muzzle pieces and nose on head with Goop glue.
3. Create tube arms using a 2½" x 6" piece of Wheat felt. Dry brush spots on the arms with Milk Chocolate. Let dry then glue center of arms at back of metal top.
4. Glue head on metal top. Glue a ½" x 4" strip of Red felt around the neck as a collar.
5. Paint Red hearts on the glass with the opaque marker. Write 'Puppy Treats' with the White marer. Outline the left side of the letters with Red marker.
6. Bring the arms around to the front of the shaker then glue together.
Optional: Tuck two puppy biscuits in hands and glue in place. Fill the jar with small dog biscuits.

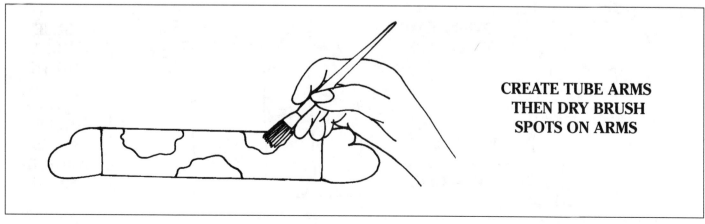

**CREATE TUBE ARMS
THEN DRY BRUSH
SPOTS ON ARMS**

19

Noah and Dove

DECOART AMERICANA PAINTS:

Fleshtone
Titanium White
Cadmium Yellow
Champagne Gold

Ebony Black
French Grey Blue
Dazzling Metallics

GLASS SHAKER:
Provo Craft #20-4211

WOOD SHAPES:
One 1½" Doll Head
Two 1⅜" x ¾" Mini Mittens
1" x 1⅛" Dove

OTHER SUPPLIES:
Williamsburg Blue Colored Felt
5" Piece of ½" Wood Dowel
6" Piece of ¼" Red/Gold Metallic Braid
White Mini Curl Doll Hair
Pink Powder Blush
Optional: Birdseed For Shaker

INSTRUCTIONS:
1. Paint head and hands Fleshtone. Dot eyes with Black. Let dry, then rub cheeks with blush.
2. Paint dove Titanium White. Shade detail lines on the dove with French Grey Blue. Dot eye Black. Paint beak Cadmium Yellow.
3. Paint dowel Champagne Gold.
4. Create tube arms using a 2½" x 6" piece of Williamsburg Blue felt.
5. Glue head on metal top. Glue center of arms to back of metal top. Drape a 3" x 12½" piece of Williamsburg Blue felt over the head. Turn back the felt ½" at the front edge then glue the felt to the top of the head.
6. Bring edges of felt together at back then glue. Glue top point of robe down. Glue headband around head. Glue curly hair beard to face. Glue bird on one hand and dowel in the other hand. Optional: Fill the shaker with bird seed.

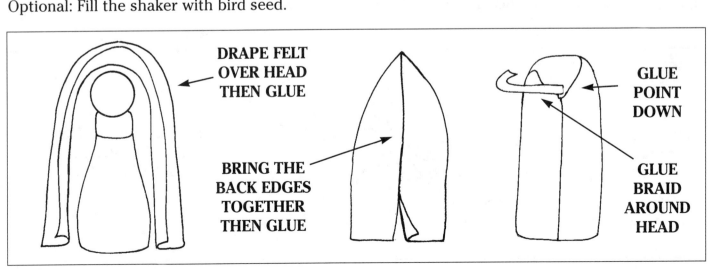

DRAPE FELT OVER HEAD THEN GLUE

BRING THE BACK EDGES TOGETHER THEN GLUE

GLUE POINT DOWN

GLUE BRAID AROUND HEAD

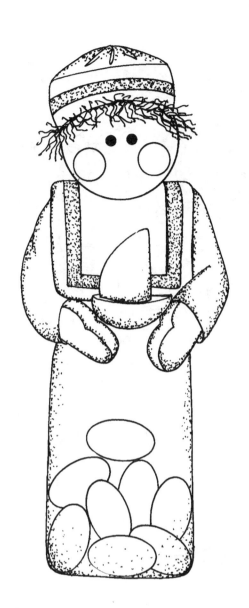

Lil' Sailor

DECOART AMERICANA PAINTS:
Fleshtone
Primary Red

GLASS SHAKER:
Provo Craft #20-4207

WOOD SHAPES:
One 1¼" Doll Head
Two 1⅜" x ¾" Mini Mittens
One ⅞" Split Wren Egg (Boat)

OTHER SUPPLIES:
Felt (White and Royal Blue)
Lil'Loopies Doll Hair - Blonde
ZIG .03 Black Millennium Marker
Lo-Temp Glue
Pink Powder Blush
18" of ⅛" Red Ribbon
Optional: Blue Jelly Beans

SAIL PATTERN

INSTRUCTIONS:
1. Paint the head and hands Fleshtone. Dot the eyes with Black marker. Rub the cheeks with blush.
2. Paint the split egg Primary Red.
3. Cut the collar of White felt using the pattern provided. Glue Red ribbon around the collar as shown in the illustration. Glue the collar over the metal cap.
4. Glue head on top of collar. Glue hair on head.
5. Create two sleeves using a 2½" x 2" piece of Royal Blue felt for each sleeve. Glue sleeves at sides of metal cap.
6. Gather the top edge of a 2" x 5" piece of White felt. Pull up gathers tightly then tie off. Overlap then glue back edges of felt together. Turn hat inside out. Fold back about ⅜" of the bottom edge to create a brim.
7. Glue Red ribbon around the brim. Glue the hat on the head.
8. Cut two pieces of White felt and glue together for the sail using the pattern provided. Glue the sail to the boat, then the boat in the doll's hands.
Optional: Fill the shaker with Blue jelly beans or other Blue candy.

GATHER TOP EDGE OF FELT. TURN HAT INSIDE OUT AND BRIM UPWARDS

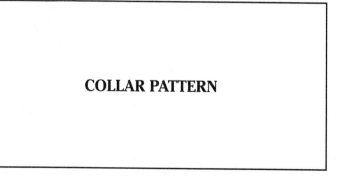

COLLAR PATTERN

Teacher Time

DECOART AMERICANA PAINTS:
Buttermilk   Cadmium Yellow
Fleshtone   Primary Red
Sapphire   Viridian Green

GLASS SHAKER:
Provo Craft #20-4211

WOOD SHAPES:
One 1½" Ball Head
Two 1⅜" x ¾" Mittens
Mini Book Assortment
½" Micro Apple

OTHER SUPPLIES:
Williamsburg Blue Felt
Rust Lil'Loopies Doll Hair
4" White Crocheted Doily
3" x 3½" Piece of Red Print Cotton Fabric
½" x 6" Piece of Red Print Cotton Fabric
Small Green Silk Leaf
Pink Powder Blush
ZIG .03 Black Millennium Marker
Lo-Temp Glue
Needle and Red Thread
Optional: White Chalk for Shaker

INSTRUCTIONS:
1. Paint the head and hands Fleshtone. Dot eyes and draw the mouth with Black marker. Rub the cheeks with blush.
2. Paint one book Viridian Green, one Sapphire and one Cadmium Yellow. Paint Buttermilk labels on each of the books. Write titles on each label with the Black marker.
3. Paint the apple Primary Red. Glue a Green silk leaf at the top.
4. Create two sleeves using a 2½" x 2" piece of Williamsburg Blue felt for each.
5. Gather the 2" edge of the Red fabric. Glue across the front of the metal cap as an apron.
6. Cut a 2" piece (or two crocheted scallops) from the doily then glue on metal cap as a collar. Glue the head on the cap. Glue the arms at the sides of the collar.
7. Glue the books in a stack with the apple at the top then glue the stack in the doll's hands.
8. Glue doll hair on the head, then a Red fabric bow in the hair.
Optional: Fill the shaker with white chalk.

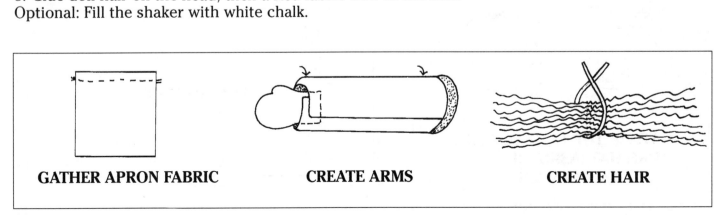

GATHER APRON FABRIC   **CREATE ARMS**   **CREATE HAIR**

spice Girl

DECOART AMERICANA PAINTS:
Hauser Medium Green
Milk Chocolate
Wedgwood Blue
Titanium White
Lamp Black
Primary Red

GLASS SHAKER:
Provo Craft #20-4211

APRON PATTERN

WOOD SHAPES:
One 1¼" Ball Head
Two 1⅜" x ¾" Mittens
One ⅝" x 1½" Sign
One ¾" Bowl
One 1⅝" x ⅜" Rolling Pin

OTHER SUPPLIES:
Etchall Dip'n Etch or Etching Creme
Felt (White and Cocoa)
18" of 5⁄16" Red Picot Ribbon
Pink Powder Blush
ZIG .03 Black Millennium Marker
Toothpick
Lo-Temp Glue

INSTRUCTIONS:
1. Etch shaker following basic instructions for etching glass. Paint etched glass Milk Chocolate. Paint hearts Primary Red, leaves Hauser Medium Green and 'icing' line Titanium White.

2. Paint head and hands Milk Chocolate. Rub cheeks with powdered blush. Dot eyes, cheeks and paint mouth and 'icing' lines with Titanium White. Dot pupils of eyes Lamp Black.

3. Paint sign White. Write saying on sign with Black marker. Paint handles of rolling pin Primary Red and bowl Wedgwood Blue.

4. Create tube arms using a 2½" x 6" piece of Cocoa felt. Glue the center of the arms at back of metal top.

5. Cut apron from White felt using pattern. Glue apron over metal top, then glue head on top. Tie a small Red ribbon bow then glue it on the head. Use the remaining ribbon to tie around shaker top (apron), ending with a bow at the back.

6. Glue the rolling pin to the bowl then the bowl in the doll's hands. Glue the sign to the toothpick. You may paint the toothpick if desired or leave natural. Glue the toothpick and sign in one arm.

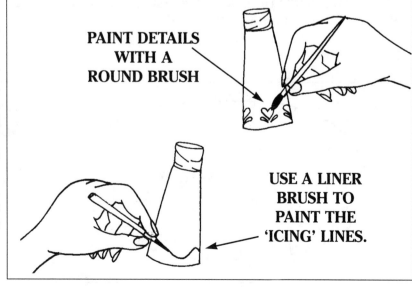

PAINT DETAILS WITH A ROUND BRUSH

USE A LINER BRUSH TO PAINT THE 'ICING' LINES.

One Little Indian

DECOART AMERICANA PAINTS:
Fleshtone

GLASS SHAKER:
Provo Craft #20-4212

WOOD SHAPES:
One 1⅝" Ball Head
Two 1⅜" x ¾" Mittens

OTHER SUPPLIES:
Camel Colored Felt
Black Wavy Wool Hair
Pink Powder Blush
ZIG .03 Black and Red Millennium Markers
Package of Covered Elastic Pony Tail Bands
Assorted Seed Beads
Beading Wire or Thread
Beading Needle
Lo-Temp Glue

INSTRUCTIONS:
1. Paint the head and hands Fleshtone. Dot the eyes with Black marker then draw the mouth with Red marker. Rub the cheeks with blush.
2. Cut the collar from Camel felt using the pattern provided. Cut fringe around the edge of the collar. Glue the collar, then the head on the shaker top.
3. Create two arms using a 2½" x 2" piece of Camel colored felt for each. Glue the arms at the sides of metal top.
4. Use covered pony tail elastics to create a design at the center of the shaker. Stretch each band onto the shaker, creating a design of your choice. Stretch two more bands around the top of the shaker, just under the lid.
5. Fluff the hair, then glue it on the head. Braid the hair at the sides of the head. Tie each braid with floss or thread. Stretch an additional band around the head as a headband.
6. String the beads to make a necklace. Assemble the necklace around the doll's neck. Fill the container with the remaining pony tail bands.

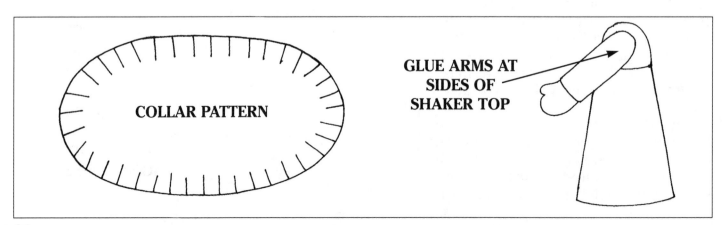

COLLAR PATTERN

GLUE ARMS AT SIDES OF SHAKER TOP

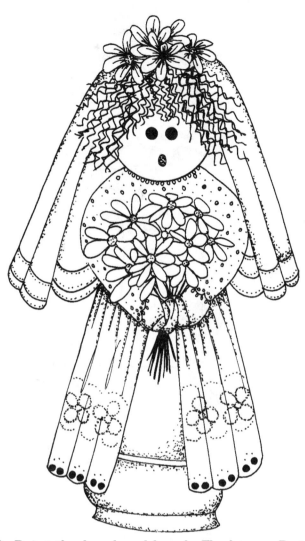

The Bride

DECOART AMERICANA PAINTS:
Fleshtone

GLASS SHAKER:
Provo Craft #20-4212

WOOD SHAPES:
One 1¼" Ball Head
Two 1⅜" x ¾" Mittens

OTHER SUPPLIES:
Etchall Dip'n Etch or Etching Creme
4" x 8" Piece of White Lace For Dress
4" x 5" Piece of White Lace for Veil
2" x 6" Piece of Lace for Arms
5" of 1" Gathered White Ribbon and Lace Trim
Small Bundle of White Silk Flowers
Blonde Lil'Loopies Doll Hair
Pink Powder Blush
ZIG .03 Black and Red Millennium Marker
Needle and Thread (White)
Lo-Temp Glue
Optional: Rice to Fill Shaker

INSTRUCTIONS:
1. Etch shaker following basic instructions for etching glass.
2. Paint the head and hands Fleshtone. Dot the eyes with Black marker and the mouth with Red marker. Rub cheeks with blush.
3. Glue head on metal top.
4. Gather the top edge of dress lace. Turn under ¼" on each short side then glue. Pull up gathering threads tightly, then assemble and glue dress on doll. Glue the gathered ribbon and lace around the doll's neck for a collar.
5. Fold longest raw edges of arm lace to meet at the center. Fold lace in half again then glue folded edges together with the hands glued at the ends. Glue the center of arms at back of dress, adjusting length of arms if necessary. Glue a small bunch of flowers in doll's hands.
6. Glue hair on head. Gather top edge of veil. Fold short edges under ¼" then glue. Pull up gathering threads tightly then glue veil on head. Glue White silk flowers at top of veil.
Optional: Fill shaker with rice.

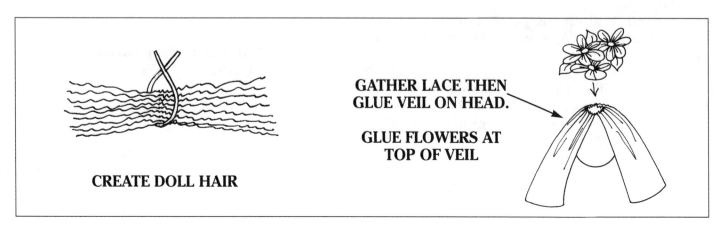

CREATE DOLL HAIR

GATHER LACE THEN GLUE VEIL ON HEAD.

GLUE FLOWERS AT TOP OF VEIL

The Groom

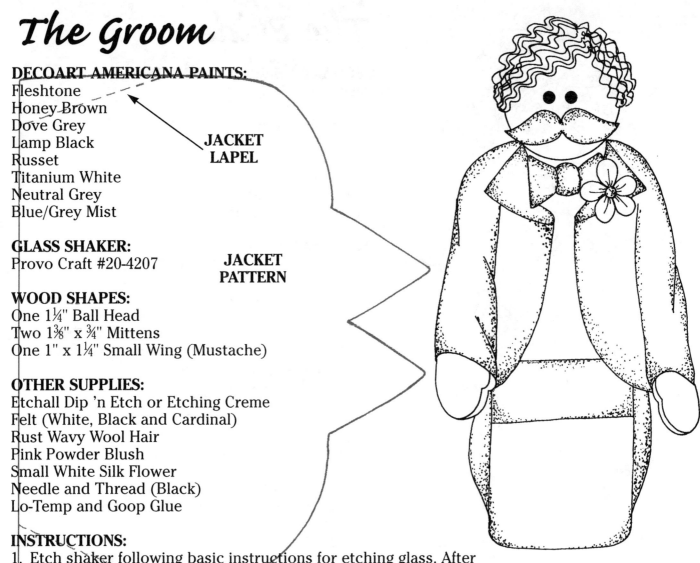

JACKET LAPEL

JACKET PATTERN

DECOART AMERICANA PAINTS:
Fleshtone
Honey Brown
Dove Grey
Lamp Black
Russet
Titanium White
Neutral Grey
Blue/Grey Mist

GLASS SHAKER:
Provo Craft #20-4207

WOOD SHAPES:
One 1¼" Ball Head
Two 1⅜" x ¾" Mittens
One 1" x 1¼" Small Wing (Mustache)

OTHER SUPPLIES:
Etchall Dip 'n Etch or Etching Creme
Felt (White, Black and Cardinal)
Rust Wavy Wool Hair
Pink Powder Blush
Small White Silk Flower
Needle and Thread (Black)
Lo-Temp and Goop Glue

INSTRUCTIONS:

1. Etch shaker following basic instructions for etching glass. After etching, paint the bottom ½ of the shaker Blue Grey Mist and the top ½ Titanium White. Shade the edges of the Grey areas very lightly with Neutral Grey.

2. Paint the hands and head Fleshtone. Rub the cheeks with blush. Dot the eyes with Lamp Black. Paint the mustache Honey Brown. Stroke lines of Russet over the Honey Brown. Glue the mustache on the face with Goop glue.

3. Glue a 1½" x 5" piece of White felt around the metal cap, easing fullness at the top of the cap as you glue. Glue a ¾" x 6" strip of cardinal felt around the waist as a cummerbund.

4. Cut the topcoat from Black felt using pattern provided. Glue head on the metal top. Gather the top edge of the coat leaving the lapel areas ungathered. Pull up the gathers then assemble the topcoat at the doll's neck. Glue in place. Turn lapels back then glue in place.

5. Create two arms using a 2½" x 2" piece of Black felt for each. Glue arms at coat sides.

6. Cut a ¾" square of Cardinal felt. Pinch together at the center then wrap a ⅛" strip of Cardinal felt around the center to create a bow tie. Glue bow tie at neck. Glue hair on head and flower on the jacket lapel.

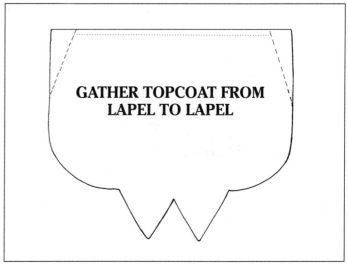

GATHER TOPCOAT FROM LAPEL TO LAPEL

Tulle Angel

DECOART AMERICANA PAINTS:
Lamp Black
Milk Chocolate
Titanium White

GLASS SHAKER:
Provo Craft #20-4206

WOOD SHAPES:
One 1" Ball Head

OTHER SUPPLIES:
Etchall Dip'n Etch or Etching Creme
1¼ Yards of 6" Wide Fine Lt. Blue Tulle
Cocoa Colored Felt
One Yard of ⅜" White/Gold Mesh Ribbon
18" of ⅛" Metallic Gold Ribbon
2" Piece of Gold Cord for Halo
Small Bundle of White Silk Flowers
Black Wavy Wool Hair
Pink Powder Blush
Needle and Thread (Blue)
Lo-Temp Glue

INSTRUCTIONS:
1. Paint head Milk Chocolate. Dot eyes Titanium White. When dry, dot pupil with Lamp Black. Rub cheeks with blush. Glue the head on the metal top.
2. Fold a ¾" x 5" piece of Cocoa felt in half widthwise to create the arms. Glue raw edges together. Set arms aside.

3. Cut a 9" length of tulle. Cut the 9" piece of tulle in half lengthwise. Wrap each end of the arms with the tulle to create sleeves. Glue ends to secure.
4. Trim the remining tulle to 4½" wide. Gather the lengthwise edge of the tulle, ⅜" from the top.
5. Pull up gathering threads tightly, then assemble the tulle around the doll's neck. Tie off threads to secure. Glue the arms at the back of the neck then bring the tulle ruffle down over the arms. Glue in place. Repeat procedure for the front ruffle collar. Starting at the center back, tie the Gold ribbon tightly around the waist (right over the metal top) ending in the front with a bow. Glue the ends of the arms together in front.
6. Glue the bouquet in the doll's hands and hair on the head. Glue the Gold cord on the head for a halo.
7. Create a six loop bow using the White mesh ribbon. Tie center of bow with thread. Glue bow at back of angel as wings.

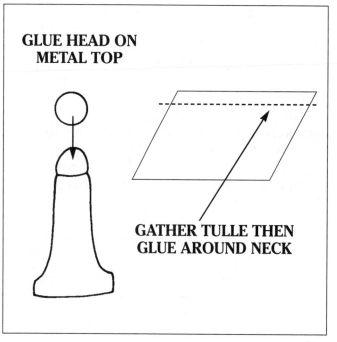

GLUE HEAD ON METAL TOP

GATHER TULLE THEN GLUE AROUND NECK

Honey Bee

DECOART AMERICANA PAINTS:
True Ochre
Lamp Black
Raw Sienna
Titanium White

GLASS SHAKER:
Provo Craft #20-4209

WOOD SHAPES:
One 1¼" x 1⅜" Crab apple (Head)
Two 1⅜" x ¾" Mittens
Two ½" Micro Apples (Antennae)
Two 1⅜" x 1⅜" Scalloped Hearts (Wings)
One 1¾" x 3/16" Circle (Collar)

OTHER SUPPLIES:
Etchall Dip 'n Etch or Etching Creme
Gold Felt
10" of 19 Gauge Black Wire
Pink Powder Blush
ZIG .03 Black Millennium Marker
14" of 19 Gauge Black Wire
Needle and Thread (Black)
Lo-Temp Glue

INSTRUCTIONS:
1. Etch shaker following basic instructions for etching glass. Paint the bee's stripes True Ochre and Lamp Black. Shade the True Ochre stripes with Raw Sienna.
2. Paint the face Titanium White, the stripe next to the face True Ochre and the back of the head Black. Shade edges of White and True Ochre area with Raw Sienna. Dot the eyes with Lamp Black. Highlight with a dot of Titanium White. Draw the mouth with the Black marker. Rub the cheeks with blush.
3. Paint the heart wings Titanium White. Shade edges with Raw Sienna.
4. Paint circle, hands and antennae Lamp Black.
5. Create tube arms using a 2½" x 5" piece of Gold felt. Glue the center of arms at the center back of the metal top.
6. Glue circle, then head on metal top. Glue heart wings at back of circle and slightly inside the arms. Bring arms to front, glue them to the metal top and glue the bouquet between the hands.
7. Bend the wire into a 'U' shape. Wrap one end around a paintbrush handle to coil it. Repeat procedure to the other side. Glue antennae (apples) on ends of wire. Glue antennae wire to top of bee with Goop glue. When dry, paint over glue with Lamp Black.

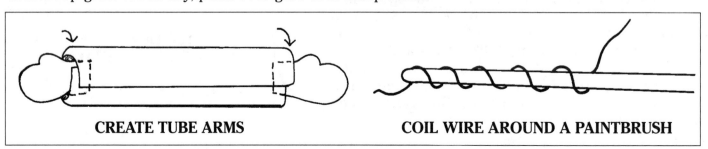

CREATE TUBE ARMS   **COIL WIRE AROUND A PAINTBRUSH**

Moo Juice

DECOART AMERICANA PAINTS:
French Mocha
Lamp Black
Neutral Grey
Titanium White

GLASS SHAKER:
Provo Craft #20-4209

WOOD SHAPES:
One 1¼" x 1⅜" Crab apple
Two ⅞" Split Wren Eggs (Hands)
One Axle Cap (Nose)
Two ½" x ⅛" Hearts (Ears)
Milk Bottle

OTHER SUPPLIES:
Etchall Etching Creme
White Felt
Pink Powder Blush
2" Straw Hat
4" White Crocheted Doily
10" of ⅛" Blue Ribbon
Small Gold Bell
¾" Burgundy Silk Rose
Two Green Silk Leaves
Lo-Temp Glue
Optional: Powdered Creamer for Shaker

INSTRUCTIONS:
1. Using a paintbrush, paint spots on glass with etching creme. Let sit 15 minutes then wash off creme under running water. Paint the etched spots Lamp Black.
2. Using heavy duty scissors, cut the hearts in half (see Basic Tips).
3. Paint the head, ears and milk bottle Titanium White. Glue the ears to the head with Goop glue. Let dry. Paint the spots and dot the eyes with Lamp Black. Shade the milk line on the milk bottle with Neutral Grey.
4. Paint the nose and hooves French Mocha. Dot the nose with Lamp Black.
5. Create tube arms using a 2½" x 6" piece of White felt. Paint Lamp Black spots on the arms. Let dry, then glue center of arms at center back of metal top.
6. Glue the doily, then the head on the metal top. Glue the rose and leaves on the hat, then the hat on the head. Glue the milk bottle in one arm.
7. Thread the bell on the ribbon then tie the ribbon around the cow's neck. Optional: Fill the shaker with powdered creamer.

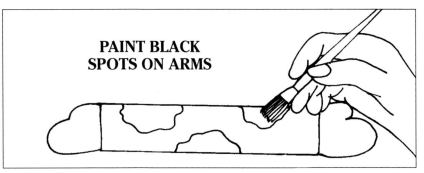

PAINT BLACK SPOTS ON ARMS

Kitchen Wishes!

DECOART AMERICANA PAINTS:

Antique White   Fleshtone
Olive Green   Sapphire
Titanium White

GLASS SHAKER:
Provo Craft #20-4211

WOOD SHAPES:
One 1¼" Ball Head
Two 1⅜" x ¾" Mittens
One Mini Bowl Assortment
One ⅝" x 1½" Mini Sign

OTHER SUPPLIES:
Felt (Turquoise, Emerald, White and Red)
Stainless Steel Dish Scrubby
⅝" Square of Yellow Sponge
12" of ¼" Ecru Satin Ribbon
Toothpick
Pink Powder Blush
ZIG .03 Black Millennium Marker
Lo-Temp Glue
Optional: Powdered Detergent

INSTRUCTIONS:
1. Paint the head and hands Fleshtone. Dot the eyes with Black marker then rub the cheeks with blush.
2. Paint the sign Titanium White. Write the saying with the Black marker.
3. Paint one bowl Olive Green and the other Antique White. Paint the toothpick Sapphire if desired.
4. Cut the apron of Turquoise felt using the pattern provided. Cut an Emerald apron pocket using the apron as a guide for size. Glue the pocket to the front of the apron, then the apron over the top of the metal cap. Tie the Ecru ribbon around the cap and the apron.
5. Create two arms using a 2½" x 2" piece of White felt for each. Glue the arms at the sides of the metal cap.
6. Glue the head at the top of the shaker. Glue some stainless steel scrubby on the head for hair. Tie a piece of Red felt around the hair as a bandanna.
7. Glue the sign to the toothpick then the sign and bowls in one of the arms. Glue the sponge at the other hand.
Optional: Fill shaker with powdered detergent.

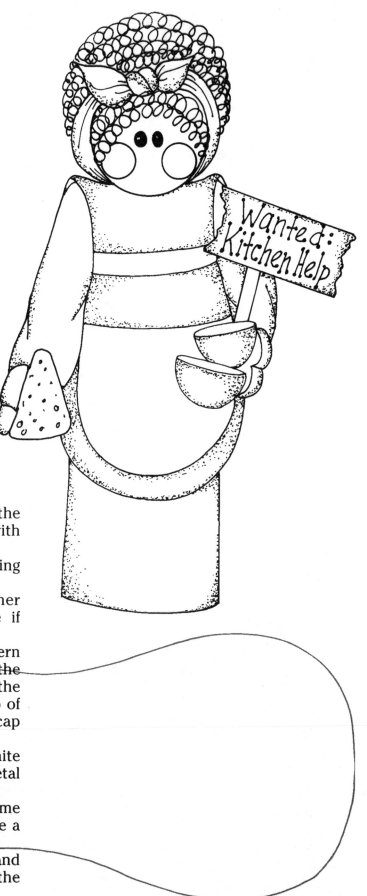

APRON PATTERN

31

Bathtime Beauty

DECOART AMERICANA PAINTS:
Fleshtone
Spice Pink
Titanium White

GLASS SHAKER:
Provo Craft #20-4212

WOOD SHAPES:
One 1¼" Ball Head
Two ½" x ⅛" Hearts
One ¾" x 1" Book
Two 1⅜" x ¾" Mittens

OTHER SUPPLIES:
Champagne Felt
Fine Mesh Pink Tulle
Blonde Mini Curl Doll Hair
Pink Powder Blush
1½" x 5½" Piece of Pink Terry Towel
Two ½" Pink Pom Poms
Four Tiny Wiggle Eyes
ZIG .03 Black Millennium Marker
Lo-Temp Glue
Optional: Pink Bath Oil Capsules

INSTRUCTIONS:
1. Paint hands and head Fleshtone. Dot eyes with Black marker. Rub cheeks with blush.
2. Paint hearts Titanium White. Mix a little Spice Pink into some Titanium White. Use the mixture to paint the bunnies' inner ears.
3. Paint the book Spice Pink and the label and pages Titanium White. Write 'Love Stories' on the label with the Black marker.
4. Create two arms using a 2½" x 2" piece of Champagne felt for each. Cut a 1¼" x 5" piece of Champagne felt then glue it around the metal top easing the fullness as you glue. Glue the head on the top and the arms at the sides.
5. Glue the terry towel around the felt covered top. Glue the book in one hand and a tuft of Pink tulle in the other.
6. Glue the hair on the head. Tie a piece of Pink tulle around the head and into a bow.
7. Glue the pom poms at the bottom front of the shaker. Glue the bunnies' ears at the top of the pom poms. Glue two wiggle eyes on each bunny. Dot the noses with Spice Pink paint.
Optional: Fill the shaker with bath oil capsules.

GLUE FELT AROUND METAL TOP EASING FULLNESS OVER THE TOP.

GLUE ARMS AT SIDES OF FELT COVERED TOP.

Cub Scout Snacks

DECOART AMERICANA PAINTS:
Cadmium Yellow
Fleshtone
French Mocha
Lamp Black
Titanium White

GLASS SHAKER:
Provo Craft #20-4212

WOOD SHAPES:
One 1¼" Ball Head
Two 1⅜" x ¾" Mittens
One ¼" Roundhead Plug (Nose)
One ⅝" x 1½" Mini Sign

OTHER SUPPLIES:
Felt (Royal Blue and Yellow)
Blonde Mini Curl Doll Hair
½" x 2¾" Piece of Self-Stick Label
Toothpick
Pink Powder Blush
ZIG .03 Black Millennium Marker
Lo-Temp Glue
Optional: Trail Mix for Shaker

INSTRUCTIONS:
1. Paint head, nose and hands Fleshtone. Shade tip of nose with French Mocha. Dot eyes with Lamp Black. Rub cheeks with blush.
2. Paint sign Titanium White. Write a saying on the sign with the Black marker. Paint the toothpick Cadmium Yellow.
3. Cut a 1¼" x 5" piece of Royal Blue felt. Glue the felt around the metal top easing the fullness as you glue. Glue the head on the metal top. Glue the hair on the head.
4. Create two arms using a 2½" x 2" piece of Royal Blue felt for each. Glue an arm at each side of the felt covered top. Tie a 3½" x 3½" x 5½" triangle of Yellow felt around the neck as a bandanna.
5. Gather one long edge of a 1½" x 5" piece of Royal Blue felt. Pull up gathering threads tightly then tie off. Glue short edges together at back. Turn hat inside out. Cut a brim using pattern provided, then glue brim to hat. Cut a ¼" Yellow felt dot then glue it to the top of the hat. Glue the hat on the head.
6. Glue the sign to the toothpick then the toothpick in one of the arms. Write a name or saying on the label then attach it to the shaker.
Optional: Fill the shaker with Trail Mix.

GLUE BRIM TO HAT

HAT BRIM PATTERN

BANDANNA PATTERN

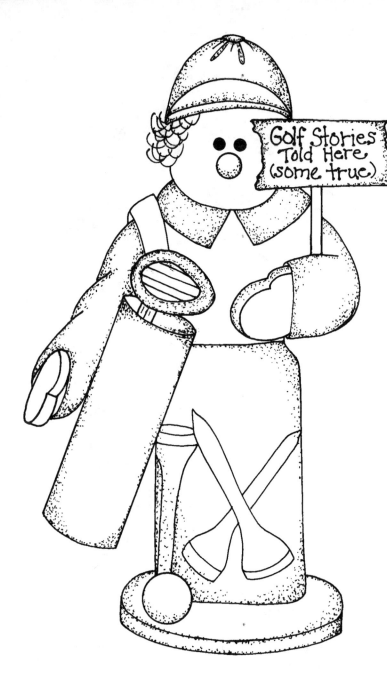

Golf Pro

DECOART AMERICANA PAINTS:

Blue Grey Mist	Fleshtone
French Mocha	Raw Sienna
Titanium White	Veridian Green

GLASS SHAKER:
Provo Craft #20-4207

WOOD SHAPES:
One 1¼" x 1⅜" Crab apple
Two 1⅜" x ¾" Mitten
One ⅞" Split Wren Egg (Club)
One ⅝" x 1½" Mini Sign
One ¼" Birch Roundhead Plug
One ½" Micro Apple (Golf Ball)
One 2⅜" x 2½" Ornament (Base)

HAT BRIM PATTERN

COLLAR PATTERN

OTHER SUPPLIES:
Felt (Royal Blue, White, Camel and Yellow)
Brown Mini Curl Doll Hair
3" Piece of ¼" Dowel
Toothpick
Pink Powder Blush
ZIG .03 and .08 Black Millennium Markers
Needle and Thread (Yellow)
Lo-Temp and Goop Glue
Optional: Golf Tees

INSTRUCTIONS:
1. Paint the head, hands and the nose Fleshtone. Shade the nose with French Mocha. Dot the eyes with Black marker then rub the cheeks with blush.
2. Paint the sign and ball Titanium White, the base Viridian Green and the dowel Blue Grey Mist. Paint the club head Raw Sienna with a Dove Grey center. Outline the Blue Grey Mist with the .08 Black marker. Write the saying on the sign with the .03 Black marker.
3. Glue a 1½" x 5" strip of Yellow felt around the metal top. Create two arms using a 2½" x 2" piece of Yellow felt for each. Glue the arms at the sides of the felt covered top. Glue the head on the metal top. Cut a collar of White felt, then glue it around the neck.
4. Gather a long edge of a 1½" x 5" piece of Yellow felt. Pull up gathering thread tightly then tie off. Glue edges closed at back then turn hat inside out. Cut a brim of Royal Blue then glue the brim to the hat. Glue a ¼" circle of Royal Blue felt at the hat top.
5. Glue the nose on the face then the hair on the head. Glue the hat on the head. Glue the sign to the toothpick then the toothpick in one arm.
6. Cut a 2" x 2½" piece and 1" circle of Camel felt for the golf bag. Overlap then glue the 2½" sides together to create a tube. Glue the circle at the bottom of the tube. Glue ¼" x 4" piece of Camel felt to the bag as a strap. Slide the strap over one arm. Glue the golf club together, then glue it in the bag.
7. Glue the shaker and the ball to the base with Goop Glue.

GLUE FELT CIRCLE AT THE BOTTOM OF GOLF BAG

Cowboy Joe

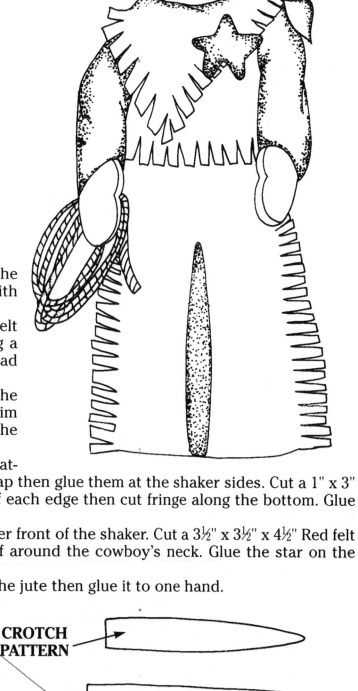

DECOART AMERICANA PAINTS:
Fleshtone
Dazzling Metallics Champagne Gold

GLASS SHAKER:
Provo Craft #20-4211

WOOD SHAPES:
One 1¼" Ball Head
Two 1⅜" x ¾" Mittens
One ¾" x ¾" Primitive Star

OTHER SUPPLIES:
Felt (Navy, Red and Camel)
Blonde Mini Curl Doll Hair
10" of 2-Ply Jute
Pink Powder Blush
ZIG .03 Black Millennium Marker
1¼" Brown Cowboy Hat
Lo-Temp Glue

INSTRUCTIONS:
1. Paint the head and hands Fleshtone. Dot the eyes with Black marker then rub the cheeks with blush. Paint the star Champagne Gold.
2. Cut a 1¼" x 5" piece of Navy felt. Glue the felt around the metal top. Create two sleeves using a piece of 2½" x 2" Navy felt for each. Glue the head on the metal top then the sleeves at the sides.
3. Cut a 4½" x 6½" piece of Camel felt to cover the shaker. Wrap the felt around the shaker then trim away excess at the back edges. Glue the felt to the shaker.
4. Cut two Camel colored felt chaps using the pattern provided. Cut fringe at the ends of each chap then glue them at the shaker sides. Cut a 1" x 3" piece of Camel felt for the waistband. Round off each edge then cut fringe along the bottom. Glue fringed felt around waist.
5. Cut the crotch of Navy felt. Glue it to the center front of the shaker. Cut a 3½" x 3½" x 4½" Red felt triangle. Cut fringe at each edge. Glue the scarf around the cowboy's neck. Glue the star on the scarf.
6. Glue the hair, then the hat on the head. Coil the jute then glue it to one hand.

BANDANNA PATTERN

CROTCH PATTERN

CHAP PATTERN

Baseball All Star

DECOART AMERICANA PAINTS:
Burnt Umber   Fleshtone
Lamp Black   Primary Red
Raw Sienna   Sapphire
Titanium White

GLASS SHAKER:
Provo Craft #20-4210

WOOD SHAPES:
One 1¼" Ball Head
Two 1⅜" x ¾" Mittens
One 2" Baseball Bat
One ⅜" Ball
One 1½" x 1¼" Folk Art Mitten (Glove)

OTHER SUPPLIES:
Etchall Dip'n Etch or Etching Creme
Felt (Red, White, Champagne and Royal Blue)
Blonde Lil'Loopies Hair
Pink Powder Blush
ZIG .03 Black Millennium Marker
Needle and Thread (Red)
Lo-Temp Glue

INSTRUCTIONS:
1. Etch shaker following basic instructions for etching glass. Paint the border at bottom of shaker Titanium White. Paint remainder of shaker Sapphire. Paint a Red sock stripe at the top of the White area. Float a shading line for the leg division on the front of the shaker.
2. Paint the head and hands Fleshtone. Dot the eyes with Lamp Black. Rub the cheeks with blush.
3. Paint the glove Raw Sienna, shade detail lines with Burnt Umber. When dry, draw the lacing lines with the Black marker. Paint the ball White. Lighten the Raw Sienna with White then paint the bat.
4. Cut a 1¼" x 5" piece of Red felt for the shirt. Glue it around the metal top, easing the fullness over the top as you glue. Glue the head on the metal top.
5. Cut a ¼" x 8" strip of White felt. Glue at the front of the shirt and around the neck. Cut a triangle of Royal Blue felt to fit at the neckline, then glue it in place.
6. Create arms using a 2½" x 2" piece of Champagne felt for each. Cut two ¾" x 2½" pieces of Red felt. Glue each one around the upper part of each arm to create a sleeve. Round off the edges of the Red felt then glue shut. Glue the arms to the sides of the shaker.
7. Gather one long edge of a 1½" x 5" piece of Red felt. Pull up gathering threads tightly then tie off. Glue edges closed at back. Turn hat inside out. Cut a hat brim of Royal Blue then glue it to the hat. Cut a letter and glue to the front of the hat.
8. Glue the hair, then the hat on the head. Glue the ball to the mit, then the mit in one arm. Glue the bat in the other arm.

GLUE BRIM TO HAT

HAT BRIM PATTERN

singing Barber

DECOART AMERICANA PAINTS:
Antique White
Fleshtone
Primary Red
Raw Sienna
Russet
Titanium White

GLASS SHAKER:
Provo Craft #20-4212

WOOD SHAPES:
One 1½" Doll Head
Two 1⅜" x ¾" Mini Mittens
One 1¼" x 1¼" Wing (Mustache)

OTHER SUPPLIES:
Etchall Etching Creme
Felt (White and Red)
Brown Mini Curl Doll Hair
Zig .03 Black Millennium Marker
Lo Temp Glue
Pink Powder Blush
1¼" x 2" Piece of Cardstock
Transparent Tape
Optional: Red Jelly Beans

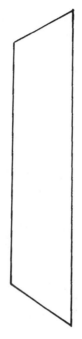

COLLAR PATTERN

INSTRUCTIONS:
1. Tape off the center of the glass shaker with transparent tape. Be sure to cover it completely so it does not etch. Spread etching creme around the detail areas at the top and bottom of the glass shaker. After 15 minutes, rinse off etching creme then remove the tape.
2. Paint etched areas White. Paint stripes Primary Red.
3. Paint the head and hands Fleshtone. Dot eyes with the Black marker, then rub cheeks with blush.
4. Paint the mustache Antique White. Paint detail lines of Raw Sienna and Russet.
5. Glue a 1½" x 5" strip of White felt around the shaker top. Create tube arms using a 2½" x 5½" piece of White felt. Glue center of arms at back of shaker.
6. Cut the collar of White felt. Glue collar around neck. Cut a ¾" square of Red felt. Pinch together into a bow tie, then wrap a ⅛" strip of Red felt around center. Glue bow tie to collar.
7. Fold the cardstock in half. Write 'Music for Quartets' and draw notes on each side of the songbook. Glue hair on head and songbook in hands. Glue mustache on face with Goop glue.

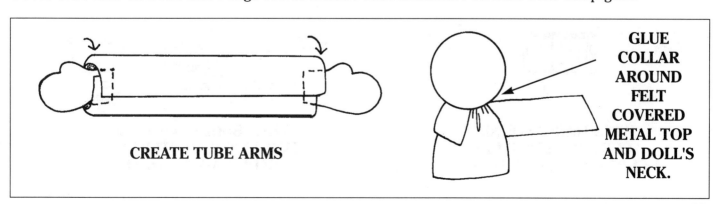

CREATE TUBE ARMS

GLUE COLLAR AROUND FELT COVERED METAL TOP AND DOLL'S NECK.

Curlers 'n Clips

DECOART AMERICANA PAINTS:
Baby Pink
Fleshtone
Titanium White

GLASS SHAKER:
Provo Craft #20-4207

WOOD SHAPES:
One 1¼" Ball Head
Two 1⅜" x ¾" Mittens
Ten ⁵⁄₁₆" x ⅜" Spools (Curlers)
One ⅝" x 1½" Sign

OTHER SUPPLIES:
Felt (White, Purple and Pink)
Blonde Lil'Loopies Hair
Pink Powder Blush
ZIG .03 Black Millennium Marker
1" Straw Basket
Toothpick
Lo-Temp Glue
Optional: Hair Clips for Shaker

COLLAR PATTERN

INSTRUCTIONS:
1. Paint the head and hands Fleshtone. Dot the eyes with Black marker. Rub the cheeks with blush.
2. Paint the sign Titanium White. Write the Saying with the Black marker. Paint the spools Baby Pink.
3. Create tube arms using a 2½" x 5½" piece of Pink felt for each. Center the arms at the back of the shaker and glue them around to the sides on the shaker top.
4. Cut a collar of Purple felt then glue it on the metal top and over the back of the arms. Glue the head on the collar.
5. Glue the hair to the head. Wrap some hair around six of the spools, then glue them across the head. Tie a White felt bandanna on the head.
6. Glue the remaining curlers in the basket. Glue the sign to the toothpick then the toothpick in the basket. Glue the basket in the doll's hands.
Optional: Fill the shaker with hair clips.

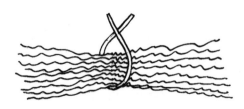

WIND HAIR AROUND CURLER THEN GLUE CURLERS ACROSS HEAD

TIE A BUNDLE OF DOLL HAIR AT THE CENTER THEN GLUE HAIR TO HEAD